A Place for Me

Including Children With Special Needs in Early Care and Education Settings

Phyllis A. Chandler

National Association for the Education of Young Children
Washington, DC

Originally published 1993 by Family Service of Omaha, 2240 Landon Court, Omaha, NE 68102–2497. 402–345–9118.

National Association for the Education of Young Children
1509 16th Street, N.W., Washington, DC 20036–1426
202–232–8777 or 1–800–424–2460

The National Association for the Education of Young Children (NAEYC) attempts through its publications program to provide a forum for discussion of major issues and ideas in our field. We hope to provoke thought and promote professional growth. The views expressed or implied are not necessarily those of the Association. NAEYC wishes to thank the author, who donated much time and effort to develop this book as a contribution to our profession.

This book was developed by the author in part with funds from the federal dependent care block grant to the Nebraska Department of Social Services, administered by Family Service of Omaha through the Nebraska Department of Education Office of Child Development.

Library of Congress Catalog Card Number: 94–065096

ISBN Catalog Number: 0–935989–59–5

NAEYC #237

Editor: Carol Copple

Original cover design: Lauren Weisberg-Norris

Design modifications and production: Jack Zibulsky

Photo credits (except p. 7 and 49): Dawn Bashara and Lauren Weisberg-Norris. These photographs were taken at the Center for Children and Children's Respite Care Center of Omaha, Nebraska.

Other photos: p. 7– © Subjects & Predicates; p. 49– © Nancy P. Alexander.

Special acknowledgment: Cynthia Kritenbrink for her research and assistance with this manuscript.

Copyediting: Dawn Bashara and Betty Nylund Barr

Printed in the United States of America

Phyllis Chandler has spent more than 25 years working professionally in the early childhood field as a teacher, director, and consultant. She holds a master's degree in child development and is an author, speaker, and consultant on children's issues and family life. She is currently a child care consultant with Family Service of Greater Omaha.

Phyllis's experience includes a variety of settings in special education and child care. Her approach to early childhood is one that considers and responds to the needs of families as well as children.

Family Service of Greater Omaha has provided child care services for more than 50 years to parents, caregivers, and corporations. In an effort to better accommodate the rapidly increasing number of working parents, the agency offers information, consultation, and training to increase the quality and availability of child care. These services include support to early childhood staff who enroll children with special needs in their program. Family Service of Greater Omaha is an affiliate member of Family Service America, a network of 300 family-serving agencies throughout the United States and Canada.

DEDICATED TO . . .

Toby, for his patience with a teacher who had a lot to learn;

Janet and her **M**om, who shared the milestones for 16 years;

Mike, whose spirit reminded me that differences don't matter;

Nicole, who at age four was a great role model for teachers;

Jeff and **E**van, who showed kids and adults what friendship is;

. . . and to the many other children and adults who taught me that the place for all of us is . . . *TOGETHER*.

Many children with special needs are enrolled in regular early childhood programs such as child care centers and preschools. Such enrollment is a wonderful learning opportunity for all concerned: adults, children with special needs, and children with typical needs. However, many staff of early childhood programs have little or no training in special education and are uncertain of their ability to teach and care for children with special needs. The purpose of this book is to provide information and support to the staff of early childhood programs and to enable them to provide a positive experience for themselves and the children in their classrooms.

CONTENTS

1

1
INTRODUCTION

3

*J*osh was a three-year-old boy with lively brown eyes, a ready smile, and dark curly hair. Each morning his mother, Barb, took him to Pat's child care class and went to her job as a nurse's aide at a nearby hospital. Barb was a single parent and Josh was her only child.

Josh spent his time at the child care center participating in activities and playing with the other children. He looked forward to going to the child care center and seemed happy there.

Pat, his teacher, was concerned about Josh. She had noticed that he walked and ran awkwardly, stumbling often. He didn't talk much and was difficult to understand. He frequently drooled. He had not yet mastered simple puzzles that were done with ease by the other children in the class.

Pat felt frustrated by these ways in which Josh differed from other, more "typical" children. Josh often needed more time than did the rest of the class to complete a task. He seemed to require more direction and closer supervision. Pat saw that Josh was not keeping up with the rest of the group. She wished he would "catch up" and be more like the other children. At times she felt angry and resentful that he was in her class.

*　　*　　*

This story describes a child with special needs. His teacher's feelings and reactions are similar to those of other early childhood staff who are responsible for the care and education of children with special needs. This book has been written especially for such teachers, to encourage and support them as they face the challenge of making the experience a successful one for the children as well as for themselves.

Who is the child with special needs?

Who exactly is a child with "special needs"? We know that all children have needs and that every child is special. However, the needs of some children are greater than or different from those of the "typical" child. For our purposes, we will define a child as having special needs if he or she is in some way outside the range of what we consider to be characteristic of a particular age. In other words, although each child is unique and children naturally differ from one another, the child with special needs differs from the average child in some way beyond that found in the normal range of individual differences.

The special need might be in the area of mental, social, emotional, or physical development. Children's disabilities vary both in form and in degree of severity. They include but are not limited to physical disabilities such as cerebral palsy or muscular dystrophy; auditory or visual disabilities; health impairments (asthma, cystic fibrosis, AIDS); developmental disabilities (mental retardation, learning disabilities); emotional disabilities; and speech/language disabilities. More than one disability may be present in a child. For instance, a child with Down Syndrome may have mental retardation, speech difficulties, and heart problems. Depending on how broadly the definition is applied, between 10% and 20% of all children may be considered to have special needs.

Some children may enter an early childhood education program before their disability has been identified. Program staff may notice that a child's development or behavior is delayed or otherwise atypical. If such a situation occurs, the program administrator should suggest to the parents that the child be evaluated by a specialist. Communication between the program staff and parents about this topic can be extremely sensitive and should always be approached with care and respect (more information regarding relationships with parents is provided in Chapter 6). Early childhood program staff may share their observations of the child's behavior but should not attempt to diagnose the problem. After the child has been evaluated, the specialist may discuss the results and recommend appropriate early intervention services if necessary.

The role of a teacher or caregiver in the identification process is to be familiar with child development, be a keen observer of children, and be familiar with community resources for appropriate referral.

Why is this child in my class?

If you are an early childhood teacher, you probably have or will have children with special needs in your classroom. Your first reaction may be, Why is this child in my class? He (or she) belongs in a special class, not in my room.

There are a number of reasons for placing children with special needs in regular programs. Legal considerations is one reason. Legislation passed in recent years at state and federal levels requires that children be educated in the "least restrictive environment" or, as the most recent legislation calls it, a "natural environment." This

means that to the extent possible, the setting in which children with special needs are educated should be the same as that in which typical children are educated. For young children, that setting is most often a regular early childhood program.

Your program will likely be affected by the requirements of the Americans with Disabilities Act (ADA). This law, which went into effect in 1992, states that people with disabilities are entitled to equal rights in employment, state and local public services, and public accommodations such as child care and early childhood education programs. The specific requirements for compliance with ADA may vary from one setting to another. For more information about ADA and how it applies to your program, see the resources at the end of this book.

The rationales for including children with special needs go beyond legal requirements:

1. Children with special needs will have better role models if they are with typical children. If they are only with other children with special needs, they have no one from whom to learn developmentally

Why is this child in my class?

7

appropriate behaviors. For example, children with speech delays are more likely to learn to talk when they are in a classroom with children who have age-appropriate language skills.

2. More realistic expectations will be placed on children with special needs who attend the same programs as children with typical behaviors and abilities. Expectations often determine how people behave and are therefore very important. For example, when children are expected to communicate their needs, they are likely to do so. If, however, an adult anticipates what a child wants and provides it without requiring any communication on the child's part, that child is less likely to develop effective communication skills.

3. Children with special needs will be perceived as less "different" if they are part of the same environment as other children; as a result they will be more readily accepted by others—their families, their peers, and the community. A child who attends ABC Early Childhood Center will be perceived as less different than one who attends XYZ Special Education Program.

4. Including children with special needs in regular early childhood programs can positively affect the development of attitudes in all children toward persons who are "different" in some way. Children learn at an early age, for example, that even though Ben can't walk, they enjoy building roads with him in the block area. As they grow older, such children are more likely to accept people with special needs in their neighborhoods, families, and workplaces.

Inclusion, or integration, of children with special needs in typical early childhood programs has value for all children. It has the potential for many positive outcomes, and doing it with thought and preparation will assist in ensuring its success.

Special services are still necessary

Integration of children with special needs into typical programs does not mean that such children do not need or will not receive special services. This is a common misunderstanding. By definition, children with special needs need special services. At times, such services may consist of extra planning by program staff or some additional training or consultation. However, the children's needs may include speech or physical therapy or other services that are beyond the scope of those found in a typical early childhood program. In such instances, it is often possible to provide the necessary special services within the regular setting rather than remove the child to a special program. In this way the child receives the benefits of inclusion, as well as the support services he needs to develop to his full potential.

A common concern of early childhood program administrators and staff is that the child with special needs will require additional resources from them—resources that the program does not have or cannot afford. How will the program provide extra help or supervision if it is required by the child? How will the needs of the other children be met if extra time and attention are given to the child with special needs? These are legitimate questions and concerns. However, such issues can generally be resolved and should be seen as opportunities for problem solving, not as reasons for denying the inclusion of children with special needs.

It is erroneous to assume that all children with special needs require extensive additional resources from program staff. This concern should not prevent a program from giving a child with special needs the opportunity to participate. Although the program must be realistic about its resources, both actual and potential, a "can do" attitude is the most important asset to successful integration of children with special needs.

Commitment, cooperation, and creativity are needed for successful integration of children with special needs in regular early childhood programs: commitment to the goal of inclusion, cooperation among those involved in services to the child and family, and creativity in resolving obstacles to successful integration of the child in the early childhood program.

2
DEALING WITH YOUR FEELINGS

*S*ue was a teacher of three-year-olds at Happy Hills Early Childhood Center. Her director had just informed her that Julie, a child with Down Syndrome, would be in her class this fall. Sue remembered meeting Julie and her parents when they visited. During that visit, Julie explored the classroom with great curiosity, excitedly pointing out things to her mother. Sue was attracted to Julie because of the little girl's friendliness, but she wasn't sure she wanted to have Julie in her room. Sue believed that she hadn't been adequately prepared to teach a child with special needs. She hadn't taken any classes in special education or had any previous experience with children with special needs. She wasn't even sure what Down Syndrome was. Could she be a good teacher to Julie? How would she know what to do? Sue was willing to try, but she wasn't convinced she could do a good job as Julie's teacher.

* * *

Sue's feelings are typical of early childhood teachers as they face the challenge of working with a child with special needs. If you are one of these teachers, you are probably experiencing the same feelings as many of your colleagues. Many of your fears and worries will disappear as you get to know the "Julie" or "Johnny" in your class. Other fears may remain or recur, and still others may develop in the future.

Your concerns are understandable and probably quite realistic. Responding to them and helping you become more confident as the teacher of a child with special needs is one of the purposes of this book.

Your feelings as you prepare yourself and your classroom for a child with special needs will probably range from resentment to enthusiasm. Taking a few minutes to identify your feelings is an important first step in the process of becoming a good teacher of children with special needs.

What have your past experiences been?

Like most adults, you have probably had some prior contact with persons with special needs. This contact may have come through family experiences, school, church, or neighborhood groups. Do you remember the little boy down the street who had braces on his legs? Or the girl in your Sunday school class who wore a hearing aid? Maybe someone in your family was in an institution and was rarely mentioned. Such previous contact has affected your attitudes toward persons with special needs. These past experiences have determined how you feel about having a child with special needs in your classroom.

Stop for a few minutes to think about your attitudes toward persons with special needs. You may want to get a pencil and paper and do this simple exercise, or you can do it mentally. Think of all the words you associate with persons with special needs. What terms come to mind? Are they positive or negative? Do they symbolize hope or pity? How would you feel if you heard these words being used to describe you?

Acknowledging what you feel is the first step in becoming a successful teacher of the child with special needs. In the following paragraphs, some of the more common feelings are identified and described.

Common feelings about persons with special needs

A frequent initial reaction to persons with special needs is to avoid or ignore them. We try not to look at the man with one arm. We hope the child with cerebral palsy won't be placed in our class. In that way, we won't have to deal with something that makes us uncomfortable. The avoidance occurs because we don't know how to respond. We are afraid we will say or do something wrong. If the child is placed elsewhere, we won't need to face the uncertainty of what to do. We think that if we don't get involved, we won't make a mistake.

Another common response is one of sadness. This is particularly so if a child was at one time normal and healthy and became disabled as the result of an accident or illness. We think about the person's lost potential. Parents of children who are born with special needs experience these same feelings as they reconcile the child of their dreams with the limitations of the real child.

Along with sadness may come a feeling of vulnerability. What if this happened to me, or to my child? Contact with children with special needs makes others more aware of "what can happen."

Denial of the problem can also occur. "He's really not retarded; he's just a little slow" or "She'll be fine as soon as she learns to talk" are characteristic responses of parents as well as teachers.

Teachers also have a tendency to believe that with enough effort, the problem can be fixed. Such feelings are especially likely when no clear cause for the disability exists. Rather than merely helping the child to learn, we want her to become "normal." Although there are situations where this can occur, they are rare. Success in teaching and caring for children with special needs cannot be measured by whether or not the child's disability disappears.

When the child does not "catch up" in spite of all the effort, several other feelings may follow. One is resentment of the child for not responding adequately to all the efforts being made ("I'm doing everything I can and she just isn't learning"). Another is guilt, or blaming oneself for not doing enough ("If I would spend more time with him, he could learn this"). Sometimes the feeling becomes one of anger, directed toward the parents, the "system," or others for not doing more to solve the problem ("I'm doing everything I can and nobody else cares").

Expect negative feelings

You will experience feelings such as these from time to time as you work with children with special needs. Although these feelings are not helpful to the children or to your work, they are to be expected. You need to accept them but not let

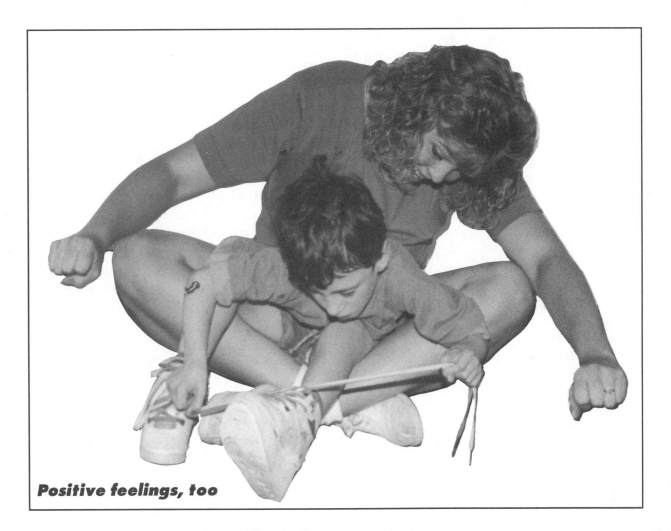

Positive feelings, too

them dominate your attitude or your efforts. The suggestions in the remainder of this book will help you take positive steps in teaching and caring for the child with special needs.

Positive feelings, too

Along with the feelings described above, you will experience positive feelings about the child with special needs. Acceptance is one of these, and it requires allowing the child to be who she is and appreciating her unique attributes. Perhaps Katie has difficulty talking, but she loves to fix "snacks" for you in the housekeeping area. Kyle can't ride a tricycle very well, but he makes wonderful drawings in the art area.

Being realistic about the child's abilities and your own strengths and limitations allows you to find effective ways to help him learn. Often, pride in yourself and the child comes as you see growth and learning taking place. You will gain new appreciation of the child and yourself as you recognize the progress that is being made toward realistic goals.

These are only some of the feelings and attitudes you may experience as you get to know and work with a child with special needs. Remember that your feelings are not good or bad; they need to be acknowledged and responded to so that you can do your best work as a teacher.

The most important fact to keep in mind is this: all children have potential and are capable of learning. Some children learn more slowly than others; some learn in different ways than others. But having the underlying belief that every child can learn will help you find effective ways to teach the child with special needs. And your appreciation of the child and of yourself will be more significant because you will recognize the effort required for that learning to take place.

3

PREPARING YOURSELF AND THE PHYSICAL ENVIRONMENT

*D*ebbie, a child care staff member, was on the playground with a group of children. Her supervisor, Ann, approached her with a new boy named Andrew. Today was Andrew's first day at the child care center. He was unable to walk or talk. Ann asked Debbie to involve Andrew in the outdoor play activities. Debbie took Andrew, and Ann went inside. Debbie had met Andrew when he arrived, but now she was panic stricken. "What do I do with him?" she wondered. "I've never been around a child who can't walk. How can he play on the playground? What if he gets hurt?" Debbie held Andrew for a few minutes and talked to him as she reflected on the situation. She had noticed earlier in the classroom that Andrew crawled quite well, so she took him to a long tunnel that was part of the play equipment. Andrew laughed delightedly as he crawled to the other end of the tunnel where Debbie was waiting for him. After they repeated this game a few times, Debbie took Andrew to a small group of children who were taking turns kicking a ball. She supported Andrew so he wouldn't lose his balance as he took his turn kicking the ball. By the time the play period was over, both Debbie and Andrew, as well as the other children, were enjoying Andrew's presence in the play group.

* * *

How would you have responded if you were in Debbie's situation? Would you have had the same feelings and concerns? Given a choice, most of us would rather not become involved in situations that make us uncertain and uncomfortable. But, like Debbie, most of us have the ability not only to handle them successfully but to increase our own growth and learning in the process.

You know a lot more than you may think you do

You probably already know more than you realize about caring for and teaching children with special needs. If you know about the development of children, you know a great deal about children with special needs because they are, first of all, children. Sometimes there is a tendency to focus primarily on the ways in which they are different. It is far more important to keep in mind that they are similar to other children in more ways than they are different from them. That is one of the reasons for using the term *children with special needs* rather than *special needs children* — they are *children* first!

If you know and understand child development, you have a great start toward working with children with special needs. Your point of reference must always be typical development. How does the behavior you are seeing compare with what is typical of normal development? In what ways does it differ? Are the behavior problems you are observing the result of a disability or just characteristic of a two-year-old? The knowledge of child development is essential to answering such questions and determining what kind of response is needed (see the Resources chapter at the back of this book).

Children with special needs may develop at a rate different from that of more typical children, but the sequence of development remains the same. For example, we know that children learn to sit before they stand, stand before they walk. This sequence is the same whether a child is nine months old or three years old. If three-year-old Amanda is unable to walk, we consider her a child with special needs. However, our knowledge of child development still tells us that she first needs to sit, then stand, before she can walk, even though her development of these skills is delayed. Again, understanding typical development provides the information needed to teach and care for the child with special needs.

Attitude is important

Your attitude toward children with special needs and their ability to learn is an important part of preparing to teach and care for them. A belief in their potential is absolutely necessary. If you believe that a child is not capable of learning, how much effort will you make to teach him? If, on the other hand, you believe that each child grows and develops at his or her own rate, you will provide opportunities for all the children in your class to do so. The next chapter will give you practical suggestions for accomplishing this goal. At present, remember that a positive attitude is the first step.

Your expectations for children are based on these two requirements described above: a knowledge of typical development and a positive attitude toward the potential of all children for growth and learning. If you possess these two attributes, you will be a successful teacher of children with special needs. All you need now is specific information about the child or children who will be enrolled in your classroom.

If this is your first opportunity to teach and care for children with special needs, it is especially important that this experience be a positive one. You may want to begin by enrolling children who have mild or moderate disabilities. Children who have severe disabilities or multiple handicaps may require more support to be successfully integrated. Children with behavioral problems also may require more resources from teachers and caregivers. See the Resources section of this book for special sources of information on teaching and caring for children with severe disabilities.

If you are uncertain that your program will be able to meet the needs of a particular child, especially one with severe disabilities, a trial enrollment period is a good alternative. This period should be at least three to four weeks long to provide adequate time for the child to adjust and for staff to assess their ability to meet the needs of all children in the group.

If you decide that your program is not appropriate for a particular child—either before enrollment or after a trial period—be sure to communi-

Attitude is important

23

cate this decision to his parents in a caring and supportive manner. Explain that your program does not have the resources to adequately meet their child's needs, rather than giving parents the impression that their child does not belong or has failed in some way. Becoming familiar with programs in your community that serve children with special needs will be helpful in enabling you to refer the family to other, more appropriate services.

A certain amount of risk is involved in accepting a child with special needs in your program, but the risk is worthwhile when it provides an opportunity for success. Ultimately, enrollment decisions must be made on an individual basis as you consider the child's needs and the resources available to help you achieve successful integration.

Meet the child

You will want to meet the child and get to know her. You might want to have her and her parents visit your program, or you might visit their home. By taking the time to become ac-

quainted with the child and her family, you will have a much clearer perception of the person involved rather than focusing primarily on the disability. In many cases this, in itself, will help you feel more comfortable with the prospect of teaching and caring for the child with special needs.

You will, of course, need some background information about the child. What is she like? What is her overall level of development? What are her strengths as well as her disabilities? The best source of this information is one or both parents. They have known their child longer and more intimately than has anyone else. Although parents may not be totally objective about their children (nor should they be), they are the best source of information about their own children. Other information may come from previous teachers, physicians, or specialists who have had contact with the child. If you are getting information from such sources, make sure you have written consent from the child's parents.

You will also want to have some information about the child's particular disability or area of special need. Many disabilities can be traced to

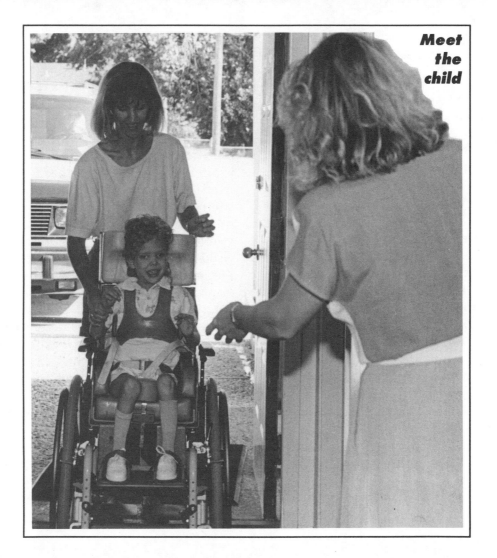

specific causes, and it is helpful to know about them (some references for further reading on particular disabilities are provided at the end of this book; other resources might be available in your community through the school system, university or college library, or advocacy organizations). In many cases, the cause of the disability remains unknown even after extensive investigation and testing.

Knowing the diagnosis of a specific problem may not provide much information about the individual child's abilities. Children with the same syndrome can have a broad range of abilities. For example, one child with cerebral palsy may be unable to walk, talk, or feed himself; in another child the cerebral palsy may only be noticeable as a slight weakness on one side of the body. Often there is a tendency to assume that all children with the same disability are similar. In fact, nothing could be further from the truth. The range of individual differences is frequently as great among children with the same diagnostic label as it is within the population in general.

Evaluate the physical environment

After you have become familiar with the child's abilities and needs, you can evaluate your program setting and make changes if necessary. Children with special needs often vary significantly in their level of development from one area to another (actually, variances among areas of development are common in all children). For example, a child's language skills may be at age level, but motor skills may be delayed by 6 to 12 months. For this reason it is easier to integrate children with special needs in groups in which a wide range of abilities is already present and accepted. The abilities of children with special needs will then fall within the range of development that is typical of other children in the class, and the classroom will provide more appropriate activities in the area of development that is delayed.

If children with typical needs are grouped according to age, a decision must be made about placement of the child with special needs who is developmentally delayed. Which class is best for a four-year-old who is developmentally at the two-year-old level? A program for four-year-olds may not seem appropriate, but is the toddler room the best placement for her? She needs to have age-appropriate peer models; she also needs to experience success in the program. Again, knowledge of the individual child will help with this decision. Perhaps the best placement would be a three-year-old classroom. Or she might be enrolled in the four-year-old room but participate in activities with younger children part of the day.

In all cases, start with a setting and program that are appropriate for the child with typical needs. Adapt your environment, materials, and activities only when such adaptation is necessary to meet the child's needs.

Questions that may apply

The following are some questions you might ask yourself as you evaluate your program environment to meet the needs of a child with a disability. After you have met the child, you will know which questions are relevant; this may vary from a few to many.

General considerations:

Are all relevant areas of the facility accessible to the child? If not, what adaptations will be made?

What is the program's policy regarding toilet learning? Will staff assist in carrying out a toilet-learning program?

Are staff physically able to provide for the needs of the child (lifting, providing closer supervision, etc.)?

Is the program able to accommodate special diets and/ or feeding needs?

If the child needs special equipment, how will it be handled (storage, access to child, staff assistance and training in its use, etc.)?

How will emergency procedures (such as fire and tornado drills) be carried out if the child requires additional support?

What provisions will be made to accommodate any special needs when children are transported on field trips?

How will information about the child's daily activities be communicated to parents if the child is unable to do so independently?

How will staff prepare for and respond to children's (and parents') questions about the child with special needs?

How will appropriate interactions between children be planned and encouraged?

How will staff encourage and respond to the nonverbal cues—such as facial expressions, gestures, and sign language—of children with communication disorders?

Are you and your staff willing (and able) to participate in carrying out the child's individualized education plan or family service plan?

How will specialists (therapists, special education staff, and others) work with the child in your program? How will space and scheduling be provided, if needed?

Health/medical considerations:

How will emergency medical situations be handled?

Do caregivers have adequate training in CPR and first aid?

Are policies regarding hygiene, medication, and illness adequate to meet the child's needs? If not, what policies need to be added or changed?

Physical considerations:

How will the child be assured of access to all activities in which other children participate (including meals and snacks, outdoor play areas, and hygiene routines)?

If any special equipment or supplies are needed, who will provide them? Who will be responsible for their care and maintenance?

Behavior/social considerations:

Are you and your staff able to provide additional support to children who need extra guidance (consider staff-to-child ratios, management techniques, more structure/supervision)?

How will you and your staff follow through on any specific behavior management techniques needed by the child?

Are you comfortable using management techniques such as behavior modification with children who need such strategies?

Considerations related to hearing:

What techniques are you and your staff willing and able to use to enhance communication with the children (such as eye contact, getting down to the child's level, gestures, facial expressions, and touch)?

Are you familiar with (or willing to learn) the communication system the child uses (for example, sign language)?

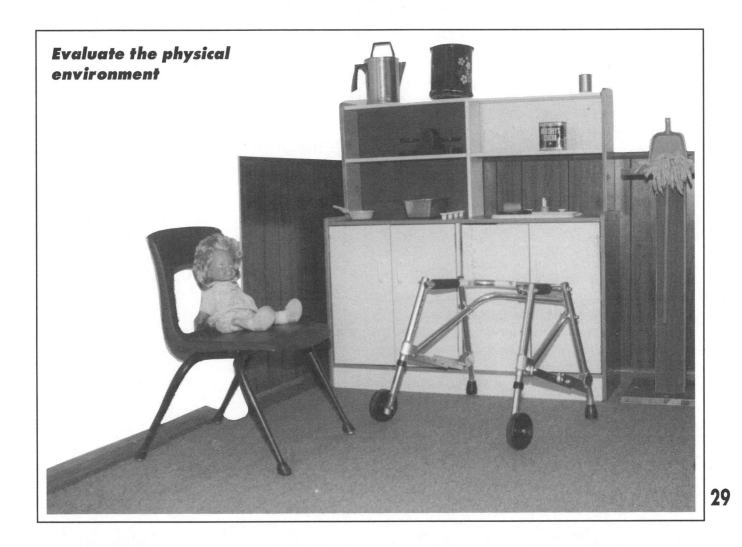

Evaluate the physical environment

29

Considerations related to vision:

How will you encourage the child to participate as fully as possible in activities in which vision is important (such as walks, books, and pictures)?

Are the routines and environment consistent and stable so the child can be as independent as possible? If changes are made, how will they be handled with the child?

* * *

Remember, you may not need to make any changes in your setting or program to accommodate the needs of a child with a disability. Very often, a good environment for children with typical needs is appropriate for children with special needs as well. The above questions are provided as a checklist for you to review *after* you have become familiar with the child who will be attending your program. You need to make adaptations only if they are indicated by the needs of that particular child.

Now—you are looking forward to this opportunity to include a child with special needs in your program. You have met the child and obtained the information you need to prepare your program. You have made any modifications in the environment that were indicated. YOU ARE READY FOR THE CHILD TO BEGIN ATTENDING. The following chapters will provide further information about making the early childhood experience in your program a positive one for you, for the child with special needs, and for children with typical needs.

31

4
THE CHILD
WITH SPECIAL NEEDS

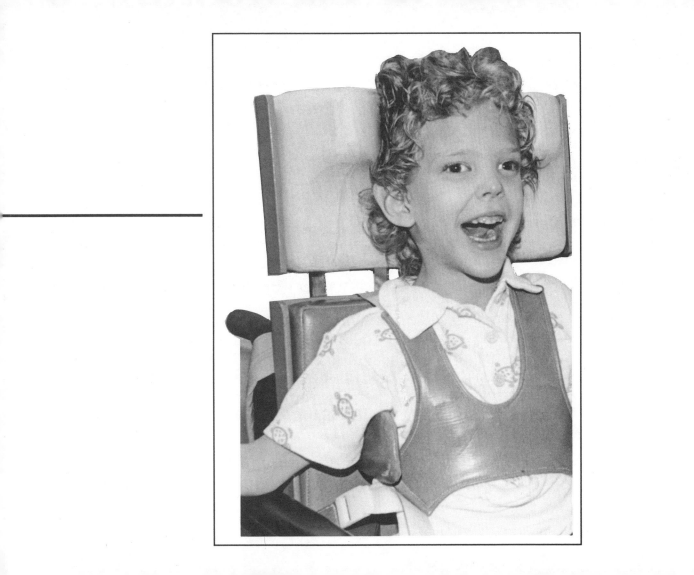

*T*he staff at Spring Street Preschool was excited about the beginning of the new school year. Four-year-old Mindy was going to be attending the morning session. Mindy was a bright and inquisitive girl who chatted readily with the teachers and other children when she and her mother visited the preschool during enrollment week. Mindy had spina bifida and had no feeling below her waist. As a result, she needed to be catheterized several times a day to prevent urinary tract infections. She wore braces on her legs and used a walker. The preschool staff were all eager to help Mindy in any way they could. They quickly realized, however, that Mindy wanted to be independent. She refused their assistance in negotiating the environment or in caring for herself. The staff learned that Mindy would not appreciate or accept their help unless she had asked for it. She didn't want special attention and took pride in doing things for herself.

* * *

Mindy obviously was a child with special needs. Yet, she clearly did not want or need to have a lot of special attention. Her greatest need was to be accepted and treated like the other children.

What does it take to successfully integrate children with special needs into regular early childhood programs? Obviously, as has been discussed, preparation is important. But once the preparation has been completed and the child begins attending, what practices will make the experience a positive one?

Children need success

It is important that the child with special needs, like all children, experience success. It may, however, be difficult without adult assistance. You may need to plan more carefully to ensure that the child with special needs succeeds in the learning activities you provide in your classroom. You also need to know how to recognize and evaluate success. Often, early childhood staff tend to compare a child with others rather than with his or her own past performance. In the anecdote at the beginning of Chapter 1, Pat felt frustrated with Josh because he wasn't doing as well as the other children in her class. She failed to notice, however, that he was steadily improving in comparison with his abilities a few months earlier. She might have perceived Josh differently if she had recognized that he was using more words and completing more difficult tasks than he had four months before.

Experiencing and acknowledging success is important to you as the teacher as well as to the child. You need to feel good about yourself and your effectiveness as the teacher of a child with special needs. Planning and identifying successful learning experiences for the child will enhance your feelings of satisfaction as his teacher.

Knowing child development is important

To help ensure that the child with special needs will have a successful learning experience, you need to know his present level of ability and how to help him learn the next step. Again, understanding child development is important. If the child is making sounds, the next step is words. If he is saying words, the next step is combining them to form phrases and short sentences. Obviously, a child who is not producing a variety of sounds is unlikely to be ready to speak in sentences. Once you have identified the next step, you can provide the experiences to support the child's learning of the skill for which he is ready.

Knowing child development will also help you to identify which behaviors are age appropriate and which ones are related to a child's disability. Is Sara having temper tantrums because she has brain damage or because she is two? Should Steven have a longer attention span or is he just acting like a typical three-year-old?

Regular activities first

In planning activities for the child with special needs, start with those that are planned for all children. Don't assume that the child with special needs requires something different. You might only need to encourage the child to participate, or give some assistance. For example, if children are dictating stories about pictures, the child who has a language delay may need more assistance and her story may not be as elaborate, but she can probably participate in the activity along with other children.

When special activities are needed, they should be planned to include other children whenever possible. If Abby needs an activity to help her learn colors, scheduling a time to play "Color Bingo" with a group of children that includes Abby will provide an appropriate activity for her *and* other children as well as social interaction for the group.

Under some circumstances, it may be necessary to plan special, separate activities solely for the child with special needs. For example, the child who is easily distracted may need individualized activities away from the group. However, this should only be done if activities with a group are not appropriate or successful.

Such special activities, when necessary, should be provided in addition to regular program activities. Taking a child to speech therapy during music time is not appropriate unless the child cannot participate at all in the regular activity. Even then, the goal should be to help him develop the skills needed to participate in the overall

activities of the program. *Special activities, if needed, should be provided in addition to, not instead of, regular program activities.* In other words, encourage the child to participate as fully as possible in activities; supplement with specialized instruction only when necessary to meet the child's needs.

Assist with integration

Children in integrated programs may need assistance with the integration process. The presence of children with special needs in regular programs is sometimes described as *physical integration*. The interaction between children with special and typical needs is called *social integration*. Although physical integration is positive and is necessary for social integration to occur, it is social integration that yields the greatest benefits. The following example will illustrate this:

Danny, *age four, attended a community early childhood center. Although his motor coordination was poor and his speech was delayed as a result of cerebral palsy, he was readily accepted by a group of boys his age. The "in" thing for this group was wearing T-shirts with their favorite TV heroes on them. One morning all his friends gathered excitedly around Danny as he arrived at the center and proudly pointed to the figure on* his *new shirt.*

Danny was physically integrated into the center simply because he was enrolled and attending there. He was socially integrated because the other boys accepted him and interacted with him as a peer. It was this social integration that provided the greatest benefit to Danny in his development.

Physical integration does not guarantee that social integration will take place. It may be necessary for you as the teacher to plan integration experiences and activities for the children. In the above example, the social integration occurred without teacher intervention, but this is not always the case. Effective ways to promote social integration will be addressed in more detail in the next chapter.

Encourage independence

It is important that the child with special needs have every opportunity to do things for herself. A common tendency is to help too much. In the example at the beginning of this chapter, Mindy let the staff know that she did not want to be helped. Many children will not communicate this as clearly. In some cases they have learned to act helpless and dependent as a means of getting attention or because they have not been encouraged to try to do things. They may not be aware of or believe in their own abilities. Doing things for them is not in their best interest. Overprotection of children with special needs seems kind, but it can be detrimental to their growth. It is far better to encourage—and perhaps sometimes to demand—that they do things for themselves and to reward them for trying. Even if they do not succeed, they have been given the opportunity to try. This risk taking is a valuable experience as long as failure is not criticized or punished in some way. The right to try gives greater dignity to children with special needs—and to other children, as well as adults.

These suggestions will help the child with special needs experience success in your early childhood program. Integration of children with special and typical needs must be a positive experience for *all* of the children if it is to be successful.

5
THE CHILDREN WITH TYPICAL NEEDS

B rent and Paul were best friends. Both four years old, they spent much of their time at the child care center playing together. They were a study in contrasts: Paul with his fair hair and blue eyes; Brent, dark haired and brown eyed. Paul was an active child who seemed to be climbing or running constantly; Brent's cerebral palsy had limited his ability to walk, run, or even sit up by himself. However, the boys had developed a rapport that was obvious to those around them. Their sparkling eyes and infectious grins told the story of their affection for one another. Through them, their families developed a relationship beyond the child care center, one that continued until Brent's family moved to another city two years later.

*   *   *

One of the major reasons mentioned in Chapter 1 for including children with special needs in typical early childhood programs is that it provides an opportunity for the development of positive attitudes among typical children and their families toward others who may be "different" in some way. This is exactly what happened between Brent and Paul and their families. Paul discovered that it was fun to have Brent as a friend, and this relationship extended to their families.

Such situations may happen spontaneously in the early childhood program where children with special and typical needs are integrated. However, the efforts of teachers and administrators can assist the process. This chapter suggests techniques that staff can use to encourage acceptance and understanding by children with typical needs.

Your attitude matters

The attitude of significant adults in the program is most important. If the program administrator is not supportive of inclusion, it is unlikely to be successful. If the teacher believes that children with special needs should be in special care and education settings, she will not support their integration in her program.

Adult attitudes are important for two reasons. First, adults provide the environment in which children learn. This is as true of attitudes and values as it is of equipment and materials. An environment in which all children are accepted and encouraged will differ greatly from one in which some children are ignored or expected to fail. In addition, children tend to imitate the behaviors of adults who are important in their lives. They will model the actions of their teachers and caregivers toward children with special needs. Compare the following two situations, for example:

It is story time. Because Jenny has a visual impairment, her teacher encourages her to sit close so she can see the pictures in the book. Later, when the children are having a puppet show, they invite Jenny to sit in front so she can see better.

It is story time. Because Erik has a hearing loss, his teacher does not expect him to pay attention, and he eventually leaves the group to wander around the room. Later, during a music activity, Erik is told to "go away" by the other children.

It is unlikely that the children's inclusion of Jenny and exclusion of Erik are just coincidences with the behavior of the teachers. It is much more probable that the children have been influenced by the attitudes and behaviors of their teachers.

Help children understand

At times, children may not have the same level of awareness that adults do about the special needs of other children. Four-year-old Mary asked her teacher if Dawn was "handicapped." The teacher, in return, asked Mary what she meant by handicapped. Mary's response was, "Those are the kids that the special teachers work with." Mary's awareness of handicaps was not based on the child's inability to walk, talk, and so forth, but on her observations of the adults who were interacting with her.

Children need to be given factual information in response to their questions. Susan, who was born with deformed fingers on one hand, had been told that they would grow as she got older. Her family believed they were protecting her feelings, but it might have been better to give her accurate information along with the assurance that she was loved and accepted just as she was.

It is important that you be matter-of-fact about differences. Give information that is as accurate and honest as possible. If you aren't sure how to answer a question, say so, perhaps adding that you will find out. As with other topics, don't overwhelm children with too much information. If they want more and feel comfortable coming to you with their questions, they will ask.

Being matter-of-fact includes what you do as well as what you say. If you are making hand prints and Susan, who has the deformed fingers, wants a turn, make prints of *both* hands, not just the one that looks normal. (If Susan is reluctant, she has already developed negative feelings about herself. Give her gentle encouragement, but if she resists, don't force her. Let her know in other ways that you accept her as she is.)

Guide understanding

As a teacher, you can help to shape the perceptions of children about persons with special needs. At times, you may need to initiate a discussion on this topic so that misconceptions do not develop. If

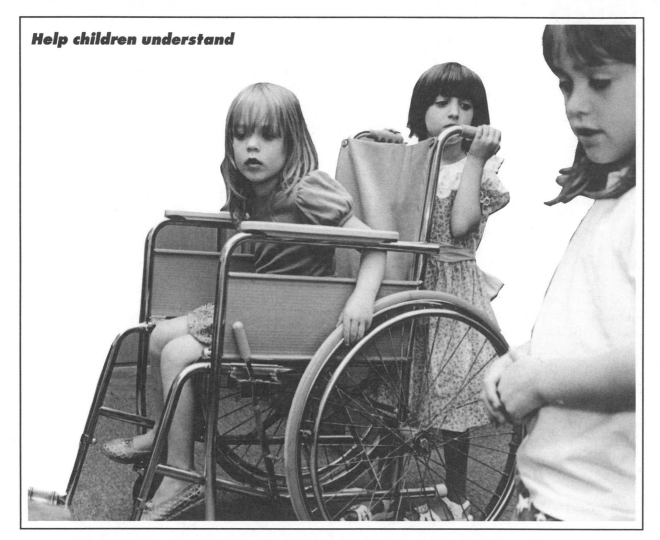

Help children understand

you notice children talking to a child who has a hearing impairment and becoming frustrated when he doesn't answer, you might say, "Tim can't hear very well. This is his hearing aid, and it helps him hear. You can help, too, by making sure he can see your face when you talk to him. If he can see you and hear some of the words, he will be able to understand you better." In this way, the children will recognize that Tim is not responding because he doesn't hear rather than because he is unfriendly.

Another way in which you can help children with typical needs develop positive attitudes toward those with special needs is to recognize and acknowledge the abilities of the child with special needs. Marc, who had a severe speech disability, was quite a mime artist, and his teachers encouraged him to share this talent with other children during drama activities.

If you observe negative behaviors, you may need to deal with them in a gentle and positive manner. Alex's friends were laughing as he imitated the way Tina, who had a congenital hip defect, walked. The teacher explained that Tina walked as she did because her bones didn't fit together the way other people's do. Alex and his friends never made fun of Tina's walk again. They weren't deliberately being cruel; they were imitating something they saw as funny. When the teacher explained, they stopped the behavior. If they hadn't, the teacher might have reminded them that it hurt Tina's feelings when they did this and asked them to stop.

The children will become more comfortable and accepting of peers with special needs if they are encouraged to examine and explore any special equipment used by the children with special needs. The following are two contrasting examples of such a situation:

Gina and Kristi, who were playing in the house-keeping area, noticed the braces that Jody wore for several hours each day. They took turns fastening the braces on themselves and trying to move in them. Then they found a doll and tried to fit the braces on her. Their teacher monitored this activ-

ity to make sure the braces weren't misused, but she allowed the two girls to explore the equipment until their curiosity had been satisfied.

Adam and Michael *noticed that Jeremy wasn't in his wheelchair. The two boys eagerly ran over to the chair and Adam began to get into it. Their teacher rushed over and said, "Get away from that chair. Don't you know that's Jeremy's chair? Leave it alone."*

Wheelchairs, walkers, and other equipment should be available for children to experiment with. Their use must be supervised so that damage will not occur, but allowing children to explore and become comfortable with such equipment is an important part of the process of understanding and accepting children with special needs. It is consistent with our knowledge that children need direct experiences for learning to be most effective. As a result, children will gain a sense of what the equipment feels like and will likely be less fearful or anxious about the apparatus and the child who depends on it.

Focus on success

Children with typical needs can also help to recognize the successes of children with special needs. When the three-year-olds were playing "Jump Over the Candlestick" and Sean, whose development was delayed due to Down Syndrome, jumped with *both feet* for the first time, the entire group cheered and clapped as excitedly as did the teacher.

Through activities such as these, the children also recognize that learning is a *process* and that children with special needs are engaged in that process, although they may be at different points. When the children notice that Annie doesn't go to the bathroom by herself, the teacher can say, "No, she doesn't yet, but today she has been dry all day and she went in the potty three times when I took her."

Plan integrated experiences

As the classroom teacher, you may need to plan integrated interactions between children with special and typical needs. A number of examples have already been given. The physical integration happens when children with special needs attend early childhood programs with other children. The social integration may need encouragement from you. You will help most by modeling the kinds of behaviors you would like to have the children learn. This has already been discussed. You can also give guidance to the children to facilitate integration. For example, if you notice that Diana is watching the children in the block area, you might say, "Diana would like to play, too. Can she help build the fence around the zoo?"

Children learn from each other. Children with special needs will often learn more from other children than from adults. That is why inclusion of children with special needs in programs with children who have typical needs is so important. The speech therapist and teachers who worked with four-year-old Chad had limited success in encouraging him to talk. On the other hand, his friend Nikki (also four) would sit next to Chad with a book, point to pictures, and say, "Ball, Chad. Say ball." And Chad would repeat the word. Next, Nikki would say, "Cookie." And Chad would say, "Cookie." And so on. Chad responded to Nikki's "teaching" very differently than he did to the therapist or teacher. The teacher encouraged and supported Nikki's friendship with Chad and her role in helping him learn.

Children with typical needs will also learn from children with special needs. Two-year-old Andrea, who wore diapers, wanted to wear panties like her classmate Jill. Their teacher explained to Andrea that in order to wear panties, she needed to start going potty in the toilet. This motivation helped make the toilet-learning process successful for Andrea. Jill was a wonderful role model for Andrea. Jill was a child with special needs; Andrea was not.

Activities designed especially for the children with special needs should include other children whenever possible. There are two reasons for this. One has already been mentioned—the other children are wonderful facilitators of learning for the children with special needs. In addition, the children with typical needs usually like to be included in special activities and may feel left out if such activities are not available to them. As children with and without special needs learn side-by-side, you can point out the positive attributes of each child, encouraging everyone to share their abilities and strengths.

A final reminder—don't overdo in your efforts to encourage acceptance of children with special needs. If you are accepting of them and relate to them in the same manner you do other children, you will already have provided most of what is needed for successful integration. After that, careful observation and occasional intervention will help you reach the goal of integration and will provide a positive early childhood experience for all the children in your program.

51

6
WORKING WITH PARENTS

*T*he four-year-old class at Sunnydale
Preschool was planning a field trip to
the zoo. Special arrangements were
made so that Martin, who used a wheelchair,
could go, too. When his mother was given the
field trip permission form to sign, she looked at
the teacher with tears in her eyes and said, "I
never imagined my son being able to go on a
field trip with regular kids."

*   *   *

Parents are an important part of any early
childhood care and education program. The
support and involvement of parents is necessary for the child's success. The more closely a
program is able to relate to and support the
role of the parents, the better able it is to meet
the needs of the child.

You are an important part of the support
system in the lives of young children. However, their lives will be most effectively en-
riched if you are able to work cooperatively
with their parents in fulfilling the responsi-
bilities of childrearing. At times, early childhood program staff tend to lose sight of the
fact that parents are the most important influ-
ence on a child's life. Respect for and support
of parents is essential to successful early childhood education.

The relationship with families of children
with special needs is even more significant
than with those of children with typical needs.
Often, the child is involved with a variety of
services, with the parent(s) having responsibility for coordination of these services. As
with any other child, parents are the primary
caregivers—primary in the sense that they
are the first, primary also because they are
the most important. Providers of early care
and education services need to keep this fact
uppermost in their minds as they work with
young children.

Parents of children with special needs

The parents of children with special needs often experience greater levels of stress in their lives than do other parents (Turnbull, Summers, & Brotherson, 1983*). In some cases, this stress leads to divorce, child abuse, or other negative outcomes. The family often has larger financial burdens because of the child's medical needs and other expenses. The autonomy of the family may be affected by the child's disabilities: it may be difficult to take the child on family outings or to find someone to care for the child so the parents can have some time for themselves or for other activities. Siblings of children with special needs also experience greater levels of stress (Powell & Gallagher, 1993*).

It is important for you in your relationship with the family of a child with special needs to be aware that such circumstances may exist in their lives. Your understanding and support can be a valuable

---

* See citations in the Resources—Publications section—
  at the end of this book.

asset to the family. Your recognition of the strengths present in every family, as well as their needs and concerns, can make a significant difference in their ability to succeed in their parenting role.

It is often difficult for parents of children with special needs to know what to expect of their children. Most parents look forward to their child reaching developmental milestones at certain ages: sitting up at six months, walking at one year, toilet training at two, reading at six, and so forth. When children do not learn such skills at typical ages, it is difficult for parents to set appropriate expectations.

Early care and education professionals can help parents set realistic expectations for their children by sharing information about the sequence of development and helping them recognize progress as growth occurs (this is another advantage of understanding child development).

All parents enjoy hearing about their children's accomplishments. Remember to share information with the parents about their child's successes. You will be affirming their positive feelings about their child, as well as letting them know that you recognize and value their child and his achievements.

Parents of children with typical needs

The parents of children with typical needs often need support, as well, when children with special needs are enrolled in regular early childhood programs. However, there is usually more concern about this *before* the integration experience. In reality, once they and their children have participated in an integrated program, parents of children with typical needs are likely to express positive feelings. A frequent response is appreciation for their child's opportunity to know and interact with children who have special needs.

Such support from parents of children with typical needs can be ensured if a few basic guidelines are followed. First, the primary concern of parents is (and should be) their own child. As long as their child's needs are met, they will not resent the inclusion of children with special needs. If, however, they perceive that their child is being overlooked because the children with special needs demand too much of a teacher's time, they will resent the presence of such children in the classroom. The solution is, of course, to make certain that staff respond to the needs of all children in the program. The fact that some children require more staff support than do others will not be an issue if the needs of all children are met.

The enrollment of children with special needs should be handled in a routine manner to avoid unnecessary concern on the part of parents. While it is appropriate to mention in a newsletter or at a parent meeting that a child or children with special needs will be attending the program, too much emphasis can result in needless anxiety. As with the children, give factual information as requested by parents. In addition, share with them the positive outcomes you believe will result from the participation of children with special needs in the program, especially as these relate to their children.

Again, your attitudes and behaviors will be an important role model for others to follow. If your approach is positive and confident, the parents of the children in your classroom will feel comfortable with the concept of integration. If they perceive it as another opportunity for their children to grow and learn, they will support your efforts.

7
WORKING WITH
OTHER AGENCIES

*E*mily's parents enrolled her in the Middleton Child Care Center when she was 18 months old. She and her older brother attended the center full time while their parents worked. Emily's development was delayed as the result of meningitis when she was just three months old. She had been diagnosed as having a hearing loss, and her motor skills were at the 12-month level. A specialist in infant/toddler development worked with her once a week, sometimes at home and sometimes at the child care center. In addition, her parents took her to speech therapy and physical therapy at a clinic in her community.

*　　*　　*

This description is typical of the agencies and services involved with many children with special needs. It may be necessary for the family to work with a large number of community agencies in order for the child to receive all of the support services she needs and for which she is eligible. The specific agencies involved will depend on resources available in the local community, as well as the needs of the child and her family. Often, several agencies each provide a different service to the child, and the coordination of these services becomes a major responsibility for the child's family. Communication among the various providers of support services is essential if the child is to benefit fully from each one and to develop her potential.

Communication is critical

Such communication is especially important between the specialists who work with the child and the early childhood program that the child attends. If you are a teacher or director in a preschool or child care center and have enrolled a child with special needs, you should expect this communication to take place on a regular basis. The importance of this communication is illustrated by comparing the following examples:

Stacy, who had a language disability, attended a community early childhood program three days a week. She also received speech therapy twice a week at a local clinic. There was no communication between the preschool staff and the speech therapist. The preschool teachers often felt frustrated in their efforts to help Stacy develop the language skills she needed to interact more successfully with them and the other children in the preschool classroom.

Laura also had a language disability. Like Stacy, she attended an early childhood program and received speech therapy. However, the preschool teachers and speech therapist communicated regularly through notes and phone calls. The speech therapist let the preschool staff know what the goals were for Laura during therapy, and the teachers then followed through on the same goals at the preschool. In this way, Laura was encouraged to practice the skills she was learning during her therapy sessions. The early childhood staff were proud of the progress they saw Laura making and their role in helping her expand her language skills.

Expect to be involved

If a child with special needs is enrolled in your early childhood program, you should *expect* to be involved in the coordination of services and in communication regarding the child's progress and future planning. Often, the staff of early childhood programs have more contact with the child than anyone except the parents. Yet, there are times when these professionals' knowledge about the child and their potential to assist in the learning process are ignored.

Ideally, you should be invited to be part of the team that identifies what the child is able to do at present and what the focus of future goals will be. However, if this does not occur, you may need to be assertive and ask to participate in this process. You have the potential to make a significant contribution to the child's development, along with the parents and other professional staff who are involved with the family on a regular basis. In some situations, you may need to assist others in becoming aware that your knowledge and involvement are a valuable part of the services provided to the child.

Although you may need to insist that you be included, everything should be done to discourage a competitive approach to working with other professionals or with the family. Being part of a team means cooperating to achieve a common goal. By sharing with and supporting one another, you, along with the other professional staff who work with the child with special needs and his family, will help him progress to his optimal potential.

Expect to be involved

CONCLUSION

The success of including children with special needs in early childhood programs with children with typical needs depends on many factors. These include believing in the underlying value of inclusion, understanding your feelings about children with special needs and the inclusion process, careful preparation of yourself and your classroom, support of the child with special needs, assisting the integration process with all children, providing understanding and support to the child's family and to the families of other children, and working cooperatively with other agencies. This book has provided basic information on all of these areas to assist you with the process of teaching and caring for children with special needs.

More important than any technique, however, is your underlying belief in and acceptance of every child as a unique and special person with the potential to grow and develop. Your acknowledgment of this belief will enable you to enjoy and appreciate the opportunity you have to be an important part of this process.

Organizations

Alexander Graham Bell Association for the Deaf, 3417 Volta Pl., N.W., Washington, DC 20007. (202) 337–5220.

A private, nonprofit organization serving as an information resource, advocate, publisher, and conference organizer committed to finding more effective ways of teaching deaf and hard-of-hearing people to communicate orally.

American Association on Mental Retardation, 1719 Kalorama Rd., N.W., Washington, DC 20009. (202) 387–1968; (800) 424–3688.

American Foundation for the Blind, 15 W. Sixteenth St., New York, NY 10011. (212) 620–2000 (voice); (212) 620–2158 (TDD); (800) AFBLIND.

Assists blind and visually impaired persons with daily living activities and in acquiring rehabilitation services and educational and employment opportunities.

American Speech-Language-Hearing Association, 10801 Rockville Pike, Rockville, MD 20852. (301) 897–5700 (V/TT); (800) 638–8255.

Education and professional organization for speech, language, and audiology. Free public information literature is available upon request.

The Arc (formerly the Association for Retarded Citizens of the United States), 500 East Border St., Suite 300, Arlington, TX 76010. (817) 261–6003.

Serves professionals and parents by disseminating information on developmental disabilities, parent needs, and many other topics. A free catalog and brochure are available upon request.

The Association for Persons with Severe Handicaps, 7010 Roosevelt Way, N.E., Seattle, WA 98115. (206) 523–8446.

Provides advocacy for quality education and services for people with severe disabilities. Maintains a parent-to-parent communication network and a register of professional advisory contacts.

Clearinghouse on Disability Information, U.S. Department of Education, 330 C St., S.W., Washington, DC 20202–2524. (202) 205–8241.

Responds to inquiries on a wide range of topics, including federal legislation and federal funding for programs that serve the disabled. *The Pocket Guide to Federal Help for the Disabled Person* is free upon request.

Council for Exceptional Children, Division for Early Childhood, 1920 Association Dr., Reston, VA 22901–1589. (703) 620–3660.

Seeks to advance the education of exceptional children, both handicapped and gifted. Serves as an information broker and produces numerous publications.

Disability Rights Education and Defense Fund, 1616 P St., N.W., Washington, DC 20009.

Epilepsy Foundation of America, 4351 Garden City Dr., Landover, MD 20785. (301) 459–3700; (800) 332–1000; (301) 577–0100 (for Publications).

Provides free information and educational materials, support groups, referral services, and job-placement programs. Also monitors legislation.

The Exceptional Parent, 209 Harvard St., Suite 303, Brookline, MA 02146. (617) 730–5800.

Magazine providing straightforward, practical information to anyone involved with children or young adults with disabilities.

Head Start Bureau, P.O. Box 1182, Washington, DC 20013. (202) 205–8572.

Offers services to children with disabilities who meet poverty-level requirements. Check telephone directory or contact regional or national office.

Learning Disabilities Association, 4156 Library Rd., Pittsburgh, PA 15234. (412) 341–8077.

Devoted to children with learning disabilities. Offers information on publications, advocacy, and new developments.

March of Dimes Birth Defects Foundation, 1275 Mamaroneck Ave., White Plains, NY 10605. (914) 428–7100.

Catalogs are available for the list of programs and services.

National Association of the Deaf, 814 Thayer Ave., Silver Spring, MD 20910. (301) 587–1788 (office—voice and TTY); (301) 587–6262 (bookstore—voice and TTY).

Consumer advocate organization for deaf people. Serves as an information clearinghouse, sells books on deafness, and works with other organizations devoted to the deaf or disabled.

National Association for the Visually Handicapped, 22 West 21st St., 6th Floor, New York, NY 10010. (212) 889–3141.

Provides learning material—including large-print books and a monthly newsletter to assist parents of visually impaired children—and information on new techniques.

National Center for Education in Maternal and Child Health, 8201 Greensboro Dr., Suite 600, McLean, VA 22102. (703) 821–8955, ext. 254 or 265.

National Center for Learning Disabilities, 381 Park Ave. South, Suite 1420, New York, NY 10016. (212) 545–7510.

National Down Syndrome Congress, 1605 Chantilly Dr., Suite 250, Atlanta, GA 30324. (404) 633–1555; (800) 232–6372.

National Down Syndrome Society, 666 Broadway, Suite 810, New York, NY 10012. (212) 460–9330; (800) 221–4602.

Provides information to new parents through a newsletter, information packets, an annual conference, and a telephone hotline for questions.

National Early Childhood Technical Assistance System, 137 East Franklin St., Suite 500, Nations Bank Plaza, Chapel Hill, NC 27514. (919) 962–2001.

Assists states and other jurisdictions as they develop multidisciplinary, coordinated, culturally sensitive, comprehensive services for children with special needs from birth to age eight.

National Easter Seal Society, 70 East Lake St., Chicago, IL 60601. (312) 726–6200; (800) 221–6827.

Provides rehabilitation services to physically disabled persons and publishes books, pamphlets, and reprints.

National Federation of the Blind, 1800 Johnson St., Baltimore, MD 21230. (301) 659–9314 (voice only).

Provides advocacy, legal referrals, publications on employment issues, a computer bulletin board, and technical assistance. Sells aids and devices and exhibits adaptive equipment at conferences.

National Head Injury Foundation, 1776 Massachusetts Ave., N.W., Suite 100, Washington, DC 20036. (202) 296–6443; (800) 444–6443.

Assists persons with head injuries and their families in finding services and resources and facilitates the formation of family-support groups.

National Hemophilia Foundation, SOHO Building, 110 Greene St., Room 303, New York, NY 10012. (212) 219–8180.

Provides referral services and free literature on hemophilia and associated debilitating conditions.

National Information Center for Children and Youth with Disabilities, 1233 20th St., N.W., Washington, DC 20036. (202) 416–0300.

Provides free information, personal responses to questions, referrals, publications, and technical assistance to parents or professional groups.

National Mental Health Association, 1021 Prince St., Alexandria, VA 22314–2971. (703) 684–7722.

Provides referrals and free literature.

National Rehabilitation Information Center, 8455 Colesville Rd., Suite 935, Silver Spring, MD 20910–3319. (301) 588–9284; (800) 227–0216.

Office of Special Education Programs, U.S. Department of Education, 400 Maryland Ave., S.W., Room 3086, Switzer Building, Washington, DC 20202–3511. (202) 205–5507.

Administers Public Law 94–142, the Education for All Handicapped Children Act, that guarantees appropriate, free public education for children with disabilities.

Orton Dyslexia Society, Chester Building, Suite 382, 8600 La Salle Rd., Baltimore, MD 21286–2044. (410) 296–0232; (800) 222–3123.

International membership organization that disseminates information related to dyslexia and offers referrals for diagnosis, remediation, and tutoring.

Spina Bifida Association of America, 4590 MacArthur Blvd., Suite 250, Washington, DC 20007. (202) 944–3285; (800) 621–3141.

Emphasizes local support groups.

United Cerebral Palsy Associations, Inc., 1522 K St., N.W., Suite 1112, Washington, DC 20005. (202) 842–1266 (voice, TTY); (800) 872–5827 (voice, TTY).

Offers programs and services to prevent cerebral palsy and to help affected persons and their families.

U.S. Office of Special Education Programs, Early Childhood Branch, 330 C St., S.W., Washington, DC 20202. (202) 205–9084.

Provides federal financial assistance to address the special needs of children with disabilities, age birth to eight. Also assists states and local jurisdictions to improve and expand programs and services.

Zero to Three, 2000 14th St., North, Suite 380, Arlington, VA 22201–2500. (703) 528–4300.

Publishes information and sponsors conferences on infant and toddler health, mental health, and development.

Suppliers of Relevant Publications and Materials

American Action Fund for Blind Children and Adults, 18440 Oxnard St., Tarzana, CA 91356. (818) 343–2022.

Provides various services, including a lending library of children's books in both print and Braille.

Center on Human Policy/Early Childhood Direction Center, 200 Huntington Hall, Second Floor, Syracuse, NY 13244. (315) 443–3851 [Center on Human Policy]; (315) 443–4444 [Early Childhood Direction Center].

Provides books, posters, and pamphlets showing people with disabilities.

Community Playthings *and* **Rifton Equipment for the Handicapped,** Route 213, Rifton NY 12471. (919) 658–3141; (800) 777–4244; (800) 374–3866.

Quality equipment for children who are disabled.

Crestwood Company, Communication Aids, 6625 N. Sydney Pl., Milwaukee, WI 53209–3259. (414) 352–5678.

Specially adapted toys for children with special needs.

The Fibar Group, 141 Halstead Ave., Mamaroneck, NY 10543. (800) 342–2721 [in New York, (914) 835–1511].

Playground surface that makes play areas accessible for children using wheelchairs, crutches, or walkers.

Gallaudet University, 800 Florida Ave., N.E., T–6, Washington, DC 20002. (202) 651–5505 (voice and TTY).

Provides lists of organizations and programs serving the hearing impaired; hearing aid dealers; and hearing-impaired speakers who will speak at schools.

Gryphon House, P.O. Box 275, Mt. Rainier, MD 20712. (800) 638–0928.

Provides multiracial, nonsexist books that are inclusive of differently abled people.

Head Start Bureau, Resource Access Projects, Administration for Children, Youth and Families (ACYF), U.S. Department of Health and Human Services, 330 C St., S.W., Washington, DC 20201, or P.O. Box 1182, Washington, DC 20013. (202) 205–8572.

Provides curriculum and teacher training materials dealing with disability issues.

Jesana Ltd., Box 17, Irvington, NY 10533. (800) 443–4728.

Makes adapted toys and equipment for children with disabilities.

News Digest, National Information Center for Children and Youth with Disabilities, Box 1492, Washington, DC 20013. (800) 695–0285.

Newsletter presenting information on research and areas of interest, legislation, and state planning.

Sports and Spokes, **PVA Publications,** 2111 East Highland, Suite 180, Phoenix, AZ 85016. (602) 224–0500.

Magazine providing information on wheelchair sports and recreation. Will sell or loan photographs of wheelchair athletes.

Publications

Abbott, C.F., & Gold, S. (1991). Conferring with parents when you're concerned that their child needs special services. *Young Children, 46*(4), 10–14.

Presents a practical approach to sensitively, effectively working with parents of children who are developmentally delayed.

Adams, B. (1979). *Like it is: Facts and feelings about handicaps from kids who know.* New York: Walker.

Allen, K.E. (1989). *Developmental profiles: Birth to six.* Albany, NY: Delmar.

A brief yet comprehensive guide to the development of young children from birth to six years of age. Includes general information about child development, followed by selections on the infant, toddler, and preschooler, as well as age six and beyond. An excellent reference for looking at children with disabilities in the context of typical development.

Allen, K.E. (1992). *The exceptional child: Mainstreaming in early childhood education* (2nd ed.). Albany, NY: Delmar.

A resource that includes information on basic developmental milestones and typical development as well as an overview of common disabilities and their effect on children's development.

Anderson, P.O., & Fenichel, E.S. (1989). *Serving culturally diverse families of infants and toddlers with disabilities.* Arlington, VA: National Center for Clinical Infant Programs.

Talks about caring for infants and toddlers with special needs from different cultures.

Ayers, B., & Meyer, L.H. (1992, February). Helping teachers manage the inclusive classroom: Staff development and teaming star among management strategies. *The School Administrator,* 30–37.

Bailey, D.B., Jr., & McWilliam, R.A. (1990). Normalizing early intervention. *Topics in Early Childhood Special Education, 10*(2), 33–47.

This article discusses the distinction between mainstreaming and normalization. Key areas addressed are normalized environments, teaching strategies, and family-focused services in early intervention programs.

Bailey, D.B., & Wolery, M. (1992). *Teaching infants and preschoolers with disabilities* (2nd ed.). Columbus, OH: Merrill.

Baker, A.C. (1993). New frontiers in family day care: Integrating children with ADHD. *Young Children, 48*(5), 69–73.

Discusses how to help children with ADHD "fit into" a family day care environment.

Benner, S.M. (1992). *Assessing young children with special needs: An ecological perspective.* White Plains, NY: Longman.

Bordner, G.A., & Tetkowski, M. (1992). Educational play: Meeting everyone's needs in mainstreamed classrooms. *Childhood Education, 69*(1), 38–40.

An affirmation of the NAEYC philosophy of play as a child's most important work. Strategies for making this philosophy a reality in mainstreamed early childhood programs are the focus of this article.

Bricker, D.D. (1986). *Early education of at-risk and handicapped infants, toddlers, and preschool children.* Glenview, IL: Scott, Foresman.

This book focuses on practical early intervention strategies for working with children with special needs.

Brisbane, H.E. (1980). *The developing child.* Peoria, IL: Bennett.

Covers typical development from prenatal period to six years of age: physical, emotional and social, and intellectual. Also includes a special-areas section focusing on topics such as health, divorce, handicaps, and adoption.

Brown, M.H., Althouse, R., & Anfin, C. (1993). Guided dramatization: Fostering social development in children with disabilities. *Young Children, 48*(2), 68–73.

Stresses to caregivers the importance of helping children with disabilities achieve maximum independence in a supportive environment.

Carta, J.J., Schwartz, I.S., Atwater, J.B., & McConnell, S.R. (1991). Developmentally appropriate practice: Appraising its usefulness for young children with disabilities. *Topics in Early Childhood Special Education, 11*(1), 1–20.

Caston, D. (1981). *Easy-to-make aids for your handicapped child: A guide for parents and teachers.* Englewood Cliffs, NJ: Prentice-Hall. (Out of print).

How-to plans for building and customizing aids for children with special needs such as back rests, toilets, climbing frames, and walkers.

Children's Foundation. (1990). *Helping children love themselves & others: A professional handbook for family day care.* Washington, DC: Children's Foundation.

Contains an annotated bibliography of children's books and adult resources. Lists companies that supply antibias, multicultural materials. (The resource guide is also published separately.)

Cohen, D.H., Stern, V., & Balaban, N. (1983). *Observing and recording the behavior of young children* (3rd ed.). New York: Teachers College Press.

A practical guide to observation and data keeping for early childhood educators.

Cook, R.E., & Armbruster, V.B. (1982). *Adapting early childhood curricula: Suggestions for meeting special needs.* St. Louis: Mosby.

Analysis of teaching styles and strategies. Each chapter provides discussion topics, activities, and references.

Cook, R.E., Tessier, A., & Klein, M.D. (1992). *Adapting early childhood curricula for children with special needs* (3rd. ed.). New York: Macmillan.

An excellent text for anyone working with young children with special needs in the mainstreamed environment. Developmentally based with a keen view of the whole child in the context of the family, this is a practical guide for educators.

Culpepper, S. (1993). How to recognize handicaps in preschoolers. Part I: Hearing, vision, motor and language impairments, *and* Part II: Cognitive and emotional exceptionalities. *Daycare and Early Education, 20*(2), 39–43.

A concise and practical guide to detecting disabilities in young children; for early childhood educators and caregivers.

Deiner, P.L. (1983). *Resources for teaching young children with special needs.* New York: Harcourt Brace.

Resource book that examines cultural, intellectual, and physical needs. Provides ideas for curriculum adaptation and activities.

de la Brosse, B. (1987). *Children with special needs in family day care homes: A handbook for family day care home providers.* El Centro de Rosemount, 2000 Rosemount Ave., N.W., Washington, DC 20010.

Helpful information on children with special needs for day care providers (available in English and Spanish). An activity and resource book is also available.

Delventhol, M. (1991). This is my story—this is my song. *Young Children, 46*(6), 16–18.

Presents a four-and-a-half-year-old child's attempt to educate people about her epilepsy, rendered into print by her mother.

Derman-Sparks, L. (Producer). (1989). *Anti-bias curriculum* [Film]. Pacific Oaks Extension Services, 714 W. California Blvd., Pasadena, CA 91105.

Derman-Sparks, L., & the A.B.C. Task Force. (1989). *Anti-bias curriculum: Tools for empowering young children.* Washington, DC: NAEYC. Also available is a brochure for parents by L. Derman-Sparks, M. Gutiérriez, & C. Phillips, entitled *Teaching young children to resist bias: What parents can do* (1989).

Dunst, C.J., Trivette, C., & Deal, A. (1988). *Enabling and empowering families: Principles, guidelines and practices.* Cambridge, MA: Brookline Books.

Eggers, N. (1983). Influencing preschoolers' awareness and feelings regarding depicted physical disability. *Early Childhood Development and Care, 12*(2), 199–206.

Fauvre, M. (1988). Including young children with "new" chronic illnesses in an early childhood setting. *Young Children, 43*(6), 71–77.

Shows caregivers and teachers how to capably integrate children with special needs into their programs.

Fewell, R.R., & Vadasy, P.F. (1986). *Families of handicapped children: Needs and supports across the life span.* Austin, TX: PRO-ED.

Fink, D.B. (1988). *School-age children with special needs—What do they do when school is out?* Boston: Exceptional Parent Press.

Comprehensive survey of child care policy and practice for school-age children with a wide range of disabilities.

Forest, M. (1992). Full inclusion is possible. *The inclusion papers: Strategies to make inclusion work* (pp. 14–15). Toronto, Canada: Inclusion Press.

Froschl, M., Colon, L., Rubin, E., & Sprung, B. (1984). *Including all of us: An early childhood curriculum about disability.* New York: Educational Equity Concepts. (Distributed by Gryphon House, P.O. Box 275, Mt. Rainier, MD 20712).

An inclusive curriculum designed to be nonsexist and multicultural and to increase understanding of disabilities. Curriculum units include activities, materials suggestions, and well-conceived rationale and guidelines; each integrates the New Friends dolls. An extensive resource list is included.

Gallagher, J.J., & Vietze, P.M. (1986). *Families of handicapped persons: Research, programs, and policy issues.* Baltimore: Paul H. Brookes.

Goldstein, H. (1993). Use of peers as communication intervention agents. *Teaching Exceptional Children, 25*(2), 37–40.

A step-by-step guide to teaching typically developing peers to facilitate communicative interaction with socially withdrawn classmates in the early childhood setting.

Hanson, M.J., & Lynch, E.W. (1989). *Early intervention: Implementing child and family services for infants and toddlers who are at risk or disabled.* Austin, TX: PRO-ED.

Hazekamp, J., & Huebner, K.M. (1989). *Program planning and evaluation for blind and visually impaired students: National guidelines for educational excellence.* New York: American Foundation for the Blind.

Hazel, R., Barber, P.A., Roberts, S., Behr, S.K., Helmstetter, E., & Guess, D. (1988). *A community approach to an integrated service system for children with special needs.* Baltimore: Paul H. Brookes.

Heekin, S., & Mengel, P. (Eds.). (1983). *New friends.* Chapel Hill Training-Outreach Project, 800 Eastowne Dr., Chapel Hill, NC 27514.

A preschool/kindergarten curriculum designed to help teachers provide information about disabilities to young children and their families through the use of teacher-made dolls.

Heideman, S. (1989). *Caring for at-risk infants and toddlers in a family child care setting.* University of Minnesota Early Childhood Studies Program, 201 Wesbrook Hall, 77 Pleasant St., S.E., Minneapolis, MN 55455.

Discusses infants and toddlers who are at risk for neglect, abuse, or delays in normal development.

Heitz, T. (1989). How do I help Jacob? *Young Children, 45*(1), 11–15.

Describes how a kindergarten teacher who has no experience in teaching disabled children helps a child with Down Syndrome become a member of the class.

Hofschield, K.A. (1991). The gift of a butterfly. *Young Children, 46*(3), 3–6.

Tells how a butterfly that emerged from its cocoon with deformed wings became the springboard for a first grade class to learn about *people* with disabilities.

Holder-Brown, L., & Parette, H.P. Jr. (1992). Children with disabilities who use assistive technology: Ethical considerations. *Young Children, 47*(6), 73–77.

Suggests what to keep in mind when evaluating assistive technology for use with a child in your care.

Hunt, M., Cornelius, P., Leventhal, P., Miller, P., Murray, T., & Stoner, G. (1989). *Into our lives.* Tallmadge, OH: Family Child Learning Center.

A booklet designed to facilitate an understanding of the Individual Family Service Plan from a parent's perspective. Good information on the process a family goes through in integrating a child with a disability into their family.

IIg, F.L., Ames, L.B., & Baker, S.M. (1992). *Child behavior.* New York: Harper Perennial.

Classic book from the Gesell Institute of Human Development provides information about the "ages and stages" of child development from birth to age 10. Other areas of interest are covered, including fears, school issues, siblings, and discipline.

Jordan, J.B., Gallagher, J.J., Huntinger, P.L., & Karnes, M.B. (Eds.). *Early childhood special education: Birth to three.* Reston, VA: Council for Exceptional Children/ Division for Early Childhood.

Klein, N., & Sheehan, R. (1987). Staff development: A key issue in meeting the needs of young handicapped children in day care settings. *Topics in Early Childhood Special Education, 7*(1), 13–27.

Kohler, F., & Strain, P. (1993). The early childhood social skills program: Making friends. *Teaching Exceptional Children, 25*(2), 41–42.

A step-by-step guide to facilitating social interaction between typically developing young children and their peers who have disabilities.

Landau, S., & McAninch, C. (1993). Research in review. Young children with attention deficits. *Young Children, 48*(4), 49–58.

Describes how to recognize, treat, and integrate children with ADHD in early childhood programs.

Leach, P. (1992). *Your baby and child from birth to five.* New York: Alfred A. Knopf.

Focuses on development from birth to age five, with sections organized around significant areas of growth and change at each level. Addressed primarily to parents. Illustrated with drawings and photographs.

Mazzocco, M.M.M., & O'Connor, R. (1993). Fragile X Syndrome: A guide for teachers of young children. *Young Children, 49*(1), 73–77.

Describes Fragile X and characteristics of children with the syndrome.

McCracken, J.B. (1993). *Valuing diversity: The primary years.* Washington, DC: NAEYC.

Presents ideas to inspire teachers to support children's self-esteem and self-discipline, respect individual and group differences, teach children to resolve problems and conflicts peacably, and encourage cooperation.

McElroy, E. (Ed.). (1988). *Children and adolescents with mental illness.* Rockville, MD: Woodbine House.

McLean, M., & Hanline, M.F. (1990). Providing early intervention services in integrated environments: Challenges and opportunities for the future. *Topics in Early Childhood Special Education, 10*(2), 62–77.

Meisels, S., & Provence, S. (1989). *Screening and assessment: Guidelines for identifying young disabled and developmentally vulnerable children and their families.* Washington, DC: National Center for Clinical Infant Programs.

Miller, L.J., Strain, P.S., Boyd, K., Hunsicker, S., McKinley, J., & Wu, A. (1992). Parental attitudes toward integration. *Topics in Early Childhood Special Education, 12,* 230–246.

Morris, L.R., & Schulz, L. (1989). *Creative play activities for children with disabilities: A resource book for teachers and parents.* Champaign, IL: Human Kinetics Books.

A book full of ideas and practical guidance for implementing play activities in the home or early childhood education setting. The activities are applicable and beneficial for both typically developing young children and their disabled peers.

Musselwhite, C.R. (1986). *Adaptive play for special needs children: Strategies to enhance communication and learning.* Boston: College Hill Press.

A book for professionals and parents explaining how to teach developmental skills through play and promoting the use of play in all settings.

Neisworth, J.T., & Bagnato, S.J. (1987). *The young exceptional child: Early development and education.* New York: Macmillan.

Neugebauer, B. (Ed.). (1992). *Alike and different: Exploring our humanity with young children* (rev. ed.). Washington, DC: NAEYC.

Contains a collection of essays to help caregivers integrate children with special needs and from all sorts of backgrounds into their program.

Odom, S.L., & Karnes, M.B. (1988). *Early intervention for infants and children with handicaps: An empirical base.* Baltimore: Paul H. Brookes.

Odom, S.L., & McEvoy, M.A. (1988). Integration of young children with handicaps and normally developing children. In S.L. Odom & M.B. Karnes (Eds.), *Early intervention for infants and children with handicaps: An empirical base* (pp. 241–267). Baltimore: Paul H. Brookes.

Odom, S.L., & McEvoy, M.A. (1990). Mainstreaming at the preschool level: Potential barriers and tasks for the field. *Topics in Early Childhood Special Education, 10*(2), 48–61.

While affirming the value and necessity of mainstreaming young children with disabilities, this article takes a look at barriers that exist to the process (differences in ECE and ECSE philosophy, personnel preparation, etc.) and how professionals in the field can eradicate them through interprofessional collaboration.

Odom, S.L., McConnel, S.R., & McEvoy, M.A. (1992). *Social competence of young children with disabilities: Issues and strategies for intervention*. Baltimore: Paul H. Brookes.

Odom, S.L., Bender, M.K., Stein, M.L., Doran, L.P., Houden, P.M., McInnes, M., Gilbert, M.M., Deklyn, M., Speltz, M., & Jenkins, J.R. (1989). *The integrated preschool curriculum: Procedures for socially integrating young handicapped and normally developing children*. Seattle: University of Washington Press.

With an emphasis on behavioral analysis and quantitative data recording, this is a good resource for guidance in writing behavioral objectives, especially in the areas of play and socialization.

Paasche, C., Gorrill, L., & Strom, B. (1990). *Children with special needs in early childhood settings*. Menlo Park, CA: Addison-Wesley.

Ways to meet young children's special needs within programs.

Peck, C.A., Odom, S.L., & Bricker, D. (1993). *Integrating young children with disabilities into community programs: Ecological perspectives on research and implementation*. Baltimore: Paul H. Brookes.

Peterson, N.L. (1987). *Early intervention for handicapped and at-risk children*. Denver: Love Publishing.

Comprehensive overview of early childhood special education. Contains an overview, description of the special children, discussion of service delivery, and reference list.

Powell, T.H., & Gallagher, P.A. (1993). *Brothers and sisters—A special part of exceptional families* (2nd ed.). Baltimore: Paul H. Brookes.

Project Head Start. (undated). *Mainstreaming preschoolers: Eight manuals*. Washington, DC: Head Start Bureau, Administration for Children, Youth and Families.

Pueschel, S.M., Bernier, J.C., & Weidenman, L.E. (1988). *The special child: A source book for parents of children with developmental disabilities*. Baltimore: Paul H. Brookes.

Excellent tool for professionals and parents for understanding the needs of developmentally disabled children and their families.

Rappaport, L. (1986). *Recipes for fun: Play activities and games for young children with disabilities and their families* (illustrated by Ingrid Gehle). Washington, DC: Let's Play to Grow. (Out of print).

This resource is filled with ideas for games and play activities that children and adults can enjoy as they explore the world together. Adaptations for specific impairments included.

Rose, D.F., & Smith, B.J. (1993). Public policy report. Preschool mainstreaming: Attitude barriers and strategies for addressing them. *Young Children, 48*(4), 59–62.

A concise discussion of the differences in ECE and ECSE philosophy and suggestions for utilizing the strengths of both fields to provide the best environment and provide the most comprehensive services for all children in early childhood education settings. Gives suggestions for overcoming possible roadblocks to integrating children with special needs.

Ross, H.W. (1992). Integrating infants with disabilities? Can "ordinary" caregivers do it? *Young Children, 47*(3), 65–71.

Advises how to prepare your program for infants with disabilities.

Safford, P.L. (1989). *Integrated teaching in early childhood: Starting in the mainstream.* New York: Longman.

An excellent resource book for anyone in early childhood education! The foundations for the least restrictive environment in early childhood education, methods for meeting the needs of disabled children according to specific disabilities, and discussion of the issues of mainstreaming are clearly outlined and thoroughly discussed. This is an essential book for the early childhood classroom and child care setting.

Salisbury, C.L., & Vincent, L.J. (1990). Criterion of the next environment and best practices: Mainstreaming and integration 10 years later. *Topics in Early Childhood Special Education, 10*(2), 78–89.

Savage, R. (1988). *An educator's manual: What educators need to know about students with TBI.* Washington, DC: National Head Injury Foundation.

Schleichkorn, J. (1983). *Coping with cerebral palsy: Answers to questions parents often ask.* Austin, TX: PRO-ED.

Answers questions parents often ask, including those concerning medical and surgical problems and strategies for dealing with medical and dental professionals.

Schwartz, S. (Ed). (1987). *Choices in deafness: A parent's guide*. Kensington, MD: Woodbine House.

Presents essays by parents and professionals concerning cued speech and auditory-oral and total communication. Includes overviews of deafness from medical, audiological, and historical perspectives.

Seligman, M., & Darling, R.B. (1989). *Ordinary families, special children: A systems approach to childhood disability*. New York: Guilford.

Simeonsson, R.J. (1986). *Psychological and developmental assessment of special children*. Boston: Allyn & Bacon.

Smith, B.J., & Rose, D.F. (1991). *Identifying policy options for preschool mainstreaming*. (Monograph). Pittsburgh, PA: Research Institute on Preschool Mainstreaming, Allegheny-Singer Research Institute. (ERIC Document Reproduction Service No. ED 338 403)

Souweine, J., Crimmins, S., & Mazel, C. (1981). *Mainstreaming: Ideas for teaching young children*. Washington, DC: NAEYC.

Approaches and strategies for integrating children with special needs into the early childhood classroom—developing an individualized educational plan, designing the environment, and planning the curriculum.

Strain, P.S. (1990). LRE for preschool children with handicaps: What we know, what we should be doing. *Journal of Early Intervention, 14,* 291–296.

Surr, J. (1992). Public policy report. Early childhood programs and the Americans with Disabilities Act (ADA). *Young Children, 47*(5), 18–21.

Looks at specific application of the ADA in early childhood settings.

Templeman, T.P., Fredericks, H.D., & Udell, T. (1989). Integration of children with moderate and severe handicaps into a day care center. *Journal of Early Intervention, 13,* 315–328.

Thurman, S.K., & Wilderstrom, A.H. (1990). *Infants and young children with special needs: A developmental and ecological approach* (2nd ed.). Baltimore: Paul H. Brookes.

Trainer, M. (1991). *Differences in common: Straight talk on mental retardation, Down syndrome, and life*. Rockville, MD: Woodbine House.

Author draws on her personal experience as the mother of a child with Down Syndrome, now in his twenties.

Tucker, B.F., & Colson, S.E. (1992). Traumatic brain injury: An overview of school re-entry. *Intervention in School and Clinic, 27*(4), 198–206.

Turnbull, A.P., Summers, J.A., & Brotherson, M.J. (1983). *Working with families with disabled members: A family systems approach* [Monograph]. The Research and Training Center on Independent Living, University of Kansas, Lawrence, KS.

Weiss, S. (1993). *Each of us remembers: Parents of children with cerebral palsy answer questions.* Washington, DC: United Cerebral Palsy Associations.

White, B.P. with Phair, M.A. (1986). "It'll be a challenge!" Managing emotional stress in teaching disabled children. *Young Children, 41*(2), 44–48.

> Suggests how caregivers can turn the negative feelings that may accompany caring for children with disabilities into positive outcomes.

Williamson, G. (Ed.). (1987). *Children with spina bifida: Early intervention and preschool programming.* Baltimore: Paul H. Brookes.

Wolery, M., Holcombe, A., Venn, M.L., Brookfield, J., Huffman, K., Schroeder, C., Martin, C.G., & Fleming, L.A. (1993). Research report. Mainstreaming in early childhood programs: Current status and relevant issues. *Young Children, 49*(1), 79–84.

> Examines how children with special needs are being integrated into early childhood settings.

Children's books, recordings, and videos

Alexander, S.H. (1990). *Mom can't see me.* New York: Macmillan.

Aseltine, L., & Mueller, E. (1986). *I'm deaf and it's okay.* Morton Grove, IL: Whitman.

Baker, P.J. (1986). *My first book of sign.* Washington, DC: Gallaudet University Press.

> This book for hearing children about deaf people's language will open the door to new forms of communication.

Brown, T. (1991). *Someone special, just like you* (photographs by Fran Ortiz). New York: Henry Holt.

Cairo, S. (1985). *Our brother has Down's syndrome* (photographs by Irene McNeil). Toronto, Canada:

Annick Press (distributed by Firefly Books, 3520 Pharmacy Avenue, Unit 1–C, Scarborough, Ontario, Canada M1W 2T8).

Caseley, J. (1987). *Apple pie and onions.* New York: Greenwillow.

Charlip, R., & Miller, M.B. (1984). *Handtalk: An ABC of finger spelling and sign language.* New York: Four Winds Press.

Clifton, L. (1980). *My friend Jacob.* New York: Elsevier/Dutton.

Cohen, M. (1989). *See you tomorrow, Charles.* New York: Dell.

Corrigan, K. (1984). *Emily Umily* (illustrated by Vlasta van Kampen). Toronto, Canada: Annick Press.

dePaola, T. (1981). *Now one foot, now the other.* New York: Putnam.

Greenberg, P. (1954). *People aren't potatoes.* The Growth Program Press, 4914 Ashby St., N.W., Washington, DC 20007.

Greenfield, E. (1980). *Darlene.* New York: Methuen.

Haldane, S. (1991). *Helping hands.* New York: Dutton Children's Books.

Head, B., & Seguin, J. (1975). *Who am I?* Pittsburgh: Family Communications.

Heide, F. (1979). *Sound of sunshine, sound of rain.* New York: Scholastic.

Henriod, L. (1982). *Grandma's wheelchair.* Morton Grove, IL: Whitman.

Jensen, V.A. (1983). *Catching.* New York: Putnam.

Jensen, V.A., & Haller, D.W. (1977). *What's that?* New York: William Collins.

Larche, D.W. (1985). *Father Gander nursery rhymes.* Santa Barbara, CA: Advocacy Press.

Larson, H. (1978). *Don't forget Tom.* New York: Crowell.

Lasker, J. (1974). *He's my brother.* Morton Grove, IL: Whitman.

Lasker, J. (1980). *Nick joins in.* Morton Grove, IL: Whitman.

Litchfield, A. (1976). *A button in her ear.* Morton Grove, IL: Whitman.

Litchfield, A. (1977). *A cane in her hand.* Morton Grove, IL: Whitman.

Litchfield, A. (1980). *Words in our hands.* Morton Grove, IL: Whitman.

London, J. (1992). *The lion who had asthma.* Morton Grove, IL: Whitman.

MacLachlan, P. (1980). *Through Grandpa's eyes.* New York: HarperCollins Children's Books.

Peterson, J.W. (1984). *I have a sister—my sister is deaf* (illustrated by Deborah Ray). New York: HarperCollins.

Powers, M.E. (1986). *Our teacher's in a wheelchair.* Morton Grove, IL: Whitman.

Quinsey, M.B. (1986). *Why does that man have such a big nose?* Seattle: Parenting Press.

Rabe, B. (1981). *Balancing girl.* New York: Dutton Children's Books.

Rabe, B. (1988). *Where's Chimpy?* Morton Grove, IL: Whitman.

Rosenberg, M.B. (1983). *My friend Leslie. The story of a handicapped child.* New York: Lothrop, Lee & Shepard.

Roy, R. (1985). *Move over, wheelchairs coming through.* New York: Clarion.

Sargent, S., & Wirt, D.A. (1983). *My favorite place.* New York: Abingdon.

Stein, S.B. (1974). *About handicaps: An open family book for parents and children together.* New York: Walker.

Tickle Tune Typhoon. (1989). *Let's be friends* [video]. Seattle, WA: Author.
Themes of friendship, racial equality, self-health and -care, appreciation for different abilities, and environmental awareness form the core of this release.

Understanding the ADA: The Americans with Disabilities Act. (1993). Washington, DC: The Division for Early Childhood & NAEYC.

Walter, M.P. (1980). *Ty's one-man band.* New York: Four Winds Press.

Weissman, J. (1981). *All about me/Let's be friends.* Gryphon House, 3706 Otis St., Mt. Rainier, MD 20712. Book and record available.

Wolf, B. (1974). *Don't feel sorry for Paul.* New York: HarperCollins.

INFORMATION ABOUT NAEYC

NAEYC is . . .

. . . a membership-supported organization of people committed to fostering the growth and development of children from birth through age eight. Membership is open to all who share a desire to serve and act on behalf of the needs and rights of young children.

NAEYC provides . . .

. . . educational services and resources to adults who work with and for children, including

• *Young Children,* the journal for early childhood educators

• **Books, posters, brochures,** and **videos** to expand your knowledge and commitment to young children, with topics including infants, curriculum, research, discipline, teacher education, and parent involvement

• An **Annual Conference** that brings people from all over the country to share their expertise and advocate on behalf of children and families

• **Week of the Young Child** celebrations sponsored by NAEYC Affiliate Groups across the nation to call public attention to the needs and rights of children and families

• **Insurance plans** for individuals and programs

• **Public affairs** information for knowledgeable advocacy efforts at all levels of government and through the media

• The **National Academy of Early Childhood Programs,** a voluntary accreditation system for high-quality programs for children

• The **National Institute for Early Childhood Professional Development,** providing resources and services to improve professional preparation and development of early childhood educators

• The **Information Service,** a centralized source of information sharing, distribution, and collaboration

For free information about membership, publications, or other NAEYC services, call NAEYC at 202–232–8777 or 800–424–2460, or write to NAEYC, 1509 16th Street, N.W., Washington, DC 20036–1426.